D0537099

The Conquistadores

A Proud Heritage The Hispanic Library

The Conquistadores

Building a Spanish Empire in the Americas

R. Conrad Stein

Published in the United States of America by The Child's World®
PO Box 326 • Chanhassen, MN 55317-0326 • 800-599-READ • www.childsworld.com

Acknowledgments
   The Childs World®: Mary Berendes, Publishing Director
   Editorial Directions, Inc.: E. Russell Primm, Editorial Director; Pam Rosenberg, Project Editor;
   Melissa McDaniel, Line Editor; Katie Marsico, Assistant Editor; Matt Messbarger, Editorial
   Assistant; Susan Hindman, Copyeditor; Susan Ashley and Sarah E. De Capua, Proofreaders;
   Chris Simms and Olivia Nellums, Fact Checkers; Timothy Griffin/IndexServ, Indexer; Cian
   Loughlin O'Day and Dawn Friedman, Photo Researchers; Linda S. Koutris, Photo Selector
   Creative Spark: Mary Francis and Rob Court, Design and Page Production
   Cartography by XNR Productions, Inc.

Photos
   Cover: Detail showing Spanish soldiers from *Historical Mural* by Juan O'Gorman
   Cover photograph: Danny Lehman/Corbis
   Interior photographs: Archivo Iconografico, S.A./Corbis: 15, 22; The Art Archive/Dagli Orti:
   13 (National Palace, Mexico City), 21 (Musée de Château de Versailles); Bettmann/Corbis:
   12, 14, 18, 19, 25, 30, 35; Corbis: 7 (Christie's Images), 8, 29 (Bryan F. Peterson), 31 (Danny
   Lehman); Getty Images/AFP: 17 (Jorge Silva), 24 (La Industría); Getty Images/Hulton I Archive:
   26, 32; Jay I. Kislak Foundation: 27; North Wind Picture Archives: 16, 23, 28, 34.

Library of Congress Cataloging-in-Publication Data
   Cataloging-in-Publication data for this title has been applied for and is available from the
   United States Library of Congress

8   13   21   29

Chapter One

Spain and the Conquistadores

"We came [to the Americas] to serve God and the **monarch**—*and also to get rich." Bernal Díaz del Castillo, a soldier who fought under the Spanish conquistador Hernando Cortés.*

Spain was once one of the most troubled nations in Europe. In the year 711, the Moors, a Muslim people from northern Africa, invaded Spanish lands. Soon, the Moors occupied most of present-day Spain. They founded towns and built beautiful buildings. But the Christian Spaniards resented being ruled by Muslim leaders.

Gradually, Spanish kingdoms formed and fought the Moors. By the late 1200s, Christian kingdoms had greatly reduced Moorish territory in Spain. But centuries of conflict with the Moors made Spain a nation

The Moors built many beautiful buildings in Spain, including this palace at Alhambra.

Christopher Columbus kisses the hand of his sponsor, Queen Isabella of Spain, as he leaves the dock to begin his historic voyage in 1492.

of warriors. When the Moors were defeated, the warrior chiefs looked for foreign lands to conquer. In 1492, Spain sent the Italian sea captain Christopher Columbus on an amazing voyage. Columbus attempted to reach the rich trading ports in the Orient by sailing west, around the world. Instead of landing in the Orient, however, Columbus landed in what he thought was a new world—the continents of North and South America.

The warrior chiefs from Spain poured into the Americas. The chiefs were called conquistadores, the Spanish word for conquerors. Most of the conquistadores were from families who lived well but were not extremely wealthy. The common soldiers who served under the chiefs were veterans of Spanish wars. The conquistador armies fought with rifles, light cannons, and swords. Some soldiers rode on animals never before seen in the Americas—horses.

Military Adventurers

Conquistadores were military adventurers who seemed to glory in battle. They sought riches and power. They often traveled with Spanish priests who attempted to convert the people of the Americas to Christianity. Historians have summed up the goals of the conquistadores in three words starting with the letter G—gold, glory, and God. Gold, however, was their greatest passion. Legends claimed abundant gold could be found in faraway lands beyond the Atlantic Ocean. One legend told of El Dorado, a **mystical** king who powdered his body in gold dust every morning as if he were taking a bath.

Within 50 years after the voyage of Columbus, the bold conquistadores had transformed the Americas. Among the most famous of the conquistadores were Hernando Cortés, Vasco Núñez de Balboa, Francisco Pizarro, Álvar Núñez Cabeza de Vaca, Francisco Vásquez de Coronado, and Hernando de Soto.

Chapter Two

Cortés and the Conquest of Mexico

Hernando Cortés (1485–1547) was born near the Spanish city of Salamanca. His father was an officer in the Spanish cavalry. Cortés grew up better off than most of his neighbors, but he was not rich. In 1504, at the age of 19, Cortés sailed to the Americas. Eventually, he settled on the island of Cuba, where he hoped to win fame and gain a fortune.

In 1517, a Spanish ship was blown off course and touched upon shores the Spaniards had never seen before. The ship's captain reported seeing cities of stone buildings. This news excited the Spaniards in Cuba. So far, they had encountered only primitive people living in the Americas. The conquistadores hoped these cities held the treasure they most hoped to find—gold.

With 11 ships and 550 soldiers, Cortés set sail in February 1519. His fleet explored the shores and finally

The conquistadores traveled through much of North America, Central America, and South America, claiming the land for Spain.

entered a natural harbor, which the Spaniards called Vera Cruz. But the people of the coastal region did not possess the gold Cortés so eagerly sought. Through sign language, the natives told him there was plenty of gold in a city beyond the mountains to the west. What was the name of that city? The people answered, "Mexico." Cortés then acted with bold, conquistador spirit. First, he burned his 11 ships. By destroying his fleet, he erased any thoughts his crew might have of turning back.

He then set off on an incredible journey that covered more than 250 miles (402 kilometers) over rugged mountains. On several occasions, he and his men had to fight through regions where Native Americans regarded them as foreign invaders. Cortés later wrote King Charles of Spain, "There was among us not one who was not very much afraid, seeing how deep into this country we were and among so many hostile people and so entirely without hope."

Hernando Cortés led the Spaniards in their conquest of Mexico. He was the son of an officer in the Spanish cavalry.

In early November 1519, Cortés and the Spaniards looked down upon a city so marvelous that it seemed to be the kingdom of heaven. The city sat on an island in the middle of a glistening lake. In the center stood pyramids that seemed to pierce the sky. Palaces owned by noblemen radiated out from the center of the city. A system of canals, fed by lake water, brought

Tenochtitlán was the capital city of the Aztec nation. Mexico City, the capital of modern-day Mexico, was built over the ruins of the beautiful Aztec city.

goods to an enormous city market. One of Cortés's men wrote, "Some of our soldiers asked whether the things we saw were not a dream."

The city was the capital of the mighty Aztec Empire. It was called Mexico by the people of the coastal regions. The Aztecs called it Tenochtitlán (tay-noch-tee-TLAHN). The word Tenochtitlán means "place of the cactus." Aztec tradition said the capital was built centuries earlier on the spot where the people saw an eagle perched on a cactus while eating a snake. When Cortés entered Tenochtitlán, it was home to about 200,000 people. It was probably the largest city in the world at the time.

The Aztec leader, Montezuma, greeted Cortés. At first, Montezuma believed Cortés was an ancient god who had returned to claim the Aztec Empire as his own.

In the weeks to come, the Spaniards acquired a fortune in **exquisitely** crafted gold jewelry. But hostilities soon developed between the Aztecs and the Spaniards. On the night of June 30, 1520, war erupted, and Aztec armies drove the Spaniards out of their city. Many lives were lost during the battle. To this day, June 30 is called La Noche Triste ("The Sad Night") in Mexico.

Though he had lost a battle, Cortés was not defeated. He regrouped his Spanish army. He made alliances with nearby Native

Montezuma greets Cortés for the first time. At first, the Aztec ruler greeted Cortés cordially because he believed that Cortés was an ancient god returning to the Aztecs. It wasn't long, however, before the Aztecs and Spaniards were at war.

American nations that hated the powerful Aztecs. He then launched a fierce assault on the Aztec capital. The Aztecs fought bravely, but they could not withstand the Spaniards and their Indian allies. In August 1521, the Aztec capital fell to Cortés. The wonderful city that once seemed a dream to the Spanish soldiers was now a smoking ruin. The Mexico City

Cortés defeats the Aztecs. Though the Aztecs bravely defended their capital city, they were no match for the Spaniards and their weapons.

we know today was built over the ashes of the old Aztec capital.

By conquering the Aztecs, Cortés established a great Spanish empire in Mexico. He called the empire New Spain. Priests came to New Spain and converted many of the Native Americans to Christianity. Towns and magnificent churches were built. But Spanish cruelty also emerged. The Spanish king gave large grants of New Spain's best land to Cortés and his officers. The grants included the land and the people living on the land. The Aztecs and other Native Americans became slaves to their Spanish masters.

Cortés was the most successful of all the conquistadores. He was also one of the greatest commanders in military history. However, his most lasting gift to Mexico—a new race—is largely overlooked by modern Mexican scholars. The Spanish followers of Cortés

Native Americans search for gold under the watchful eyes of their Spanish conquerors. Native Americans were often mistreated by the Spaniards and many were forced into slavery.

intermarried with the Aztecs. A new race, which blended Indian and European bloodlines, emerged. The people of the new race were called the mestizos. Today, more than 9 out of 10 Mexicans are mestizos.

Mexicans celebrate their race on October 12. It is a holiday called *Día de la Raza*—"Day of the Race." This is also Columbus Day, which honors Columbus's first

Mexicans watch a parade to celebrate the Day of the Race, or Día de la Raza, a holiday in honor of their heritage.

voyage to the Americas. The Mexicans look upon him as the founder of their race. Yet, Christopher Columbus never set foot on Mexican soil. Hernando Cortés was the true father of the mestizo people. From the Mexican view, however, Cortés was a cruel conquistador who deserves no praise. In Mexico today, a statue of Christopher Columbus stands proudly in many village squares. Nowhere is there a statue of the conquistador Hernando Cortés.

The conquistadores are praised by some historians for their bravery and condemned by others for their cruelty. Often lost in historical arguments are the conquistadores' contributions to world exploration. One such conquistador explorer is Vasco Núñez de Balboa (1475?–1519).

Balboa was born in the Spanish town of Jerez de los Caballeros. He joined a Spanish expedition to South America in 1501.

Although he was from a well-to-do Spanish family, Balboa fell deeply in debt in the Americas. To escape his creditors, he once sneaked aboard a ship and hid in an empty wine barrel.

Driven by a need to explore, Balboa led expeditions into the jungles of present-day Panama. On one expedition, Native Americans told him of a huge sea that lay to the west. In September 1513, Balboa and his party became the first Europeans to see the Pacific Ocean. Reports say Balboa waded into the waters waving his sword in one hand and a Spanish flag in the other. Balboa loudly proclaimed the Pacific Ocean and all the land beyond to be property of the Spanish king.

Balboa was a Spanish patriot. But an elderly Spanish official named Pedro Arias Dávila grew jealous of Balboa's popularity with Spanish settlers. Dávila falsely accused Balboa of treason against the king of Spain. In January 1519, Balboa was beheaded in the central square of the Spanish settlement of Acla.

Pizarro and the Conquest of the Incas

Francisco Pizarro (1478?–1541) was born in the town of Trujillo, Spain. His father, a respected army officer, never married Francisco's mother. Raised by poor relatives, Pizarro never went to school and could not read or write.

In 1502, Pizarro sailed for the Americas. He served in several conquistador armies and was with Balboa in 1513, when Europeans first saw the Pacific Ocean. In 1519, Pizarro helped to establish Panama City, which served as Spain's most important Pacific port.

Native Americans told the Spaniards that the Incas, an unbelievably wealthy people, lived to the south of Panama. Pizarro launched several expeditions to find the Inca civilization. Each expedition was unsuccessful. Pacific storms damaged his ships. In some regions, the Spaniards found nothing but **impenetrable** jungle. On the coast of Ecuador, Pizarro's party was assaulted by hundreds of warriors. The Spaniards were on the brink of being killed, but they were saved when a soldier fell off his horse. The Indians had believed the horse and rider were one being. Seeing the rider separate from the horse terrified the warriors, and they retreated.

Finally, Pizarro sailed along the coast of present-day Peru.

Francisco Pizarro was the son of an army officer. His parents never married and he spent much of his childhood living with his grandparents.

There he found temples decorated with masks of pure gold and silver. He also saw the snow-covered Andes Mountains rising in the distance as if to touch the sky. Coastal people said that there, on the tops of those tall mountains, were the cities of the Incas. The Incas, he was told, had much gold.

In 1531, Pizarro returned to Peru with 180 soldiers and 27 horses. In the Andes Mountains, the Spaniards encountered the Inca Empire, the greatest nation in South America. Inca territory stretched 2,500 miles (4,023 km) along the mountain chain. The empire embraced almost 7 million people. Inca engineers built

The Incas controlled a vast territory in modern-day Peru. Cuzco (pictured in this diagram) was their capital city.

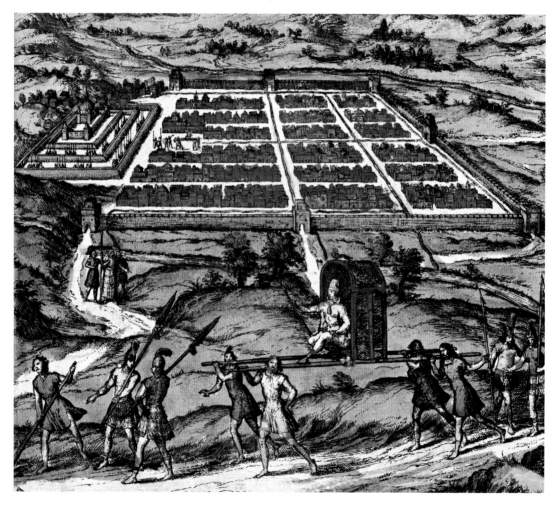

great stone cities and connected them with a complex network of roads and bridges.

In November 1532, Pizarro marched into the Inca city of Cajamarca. There he demanded to see the Inca leader. After several days, the Inca chief—a man named Atahualpa—arrived with 3,000 soldiers. A Spanish priest carrying a Bible and a flag approached

Pizarro meets Atahualpa for the first time. Imagine how surprised the Inca chief must have been when Pizarro told him that he was now a subject of Spain and must convert to Christianity.

Atahualpa. The priest informed the Inca leader that he was now a subject of the Spanish king and he must accept Christianity as his religion. Atahualpa was shocked by the Spanish demands. Witnesses said he flung the Bible to the ground. Spanish soldiers attacked the Incas. Once more, Spanish horses, firearms, and armor prevailed in battle. The Spaniards killed many Inca soldiers and captured Atahualpa.

Pizarro held the Inca emperor prisoner. The conquistador then made a fantastic demand of the Inca

The Incas filled an entire room with golden treasures such as this to meet the demands of Pizarro.

people. He entered a room in the city's palace. The room was roughly the size of a large bedroom in a modern American house. He told the Incas they must fill this room up to the ceiling with gold and silver or their leader would be killed. Historians today claim Pizarro never dreamed his demands would be met. He believed nowhere in the world was there a treasure so vast.

Over the next two months, the Incas labored to meet Pizarro's ransom orders. Workers brought the emperor's solid gold throne to the ransom room. Beautifully carved statues were taken from temples. Nobles donated gold and silver plates. Common people contributed their cherished jewelry. Incredibly, the ransom room was filled with treasure just as Pizarro had demanded. It was perhaps the largest fortune ever gathered in one spot. Still, Pizarro refused to release Atahualpa. Instead, he kept the gold for himself and his men. On August 29, 1533, Pizarro ordered Atahualpa put to death by strangulation.

Under Pizarro's leadership, Spanish armies conquered the Inca nation. Spanish settlers moved to Peru and mined gold and silver. In 1535, Pizarro founded the city of Lima and made it Peru's capital. Many historians claim Pizarro was the cruelest of all the conquistadores. The execution of Atahualpa was an act of treachery that forever condemned him as a villain. His cruelty was not only exhibited in the way he treated the Incas. He treated his own soldiers poorly. His cruelty eventually led to his own death when, in 1541, Pizarro was killed by Spanish soldiers.

Pizarro put Atahualpa in prison and demanded that a room be filled with gold or the Inca leader would be killed. Even though his demand for gold was met, Pizarro still had Atahualpa killed.

Álvar Núñez Cabeza de Vaca (1490?–1557?) was a Spanish nobleman who journeyed to the Americas when he was young. In 1528, he joined an expedition to explore what is today the U.S. state of Florida. The ship he was on was washed ashore in a storm. Shipwrecked, Cabeza de Vaca began a fantastic journey through what is now the southern United States.

On the shores of present-day Texas, he was seized and enslaved by a Native American tribe. He eventually escaped and wandered west. He hoped to reach the Pacific Ocean and spot a Spanish ship. He survived by being a trader of goods. Cabeza de Vaca picked up

colorful seashells from the coast and then hiked inland to trade the shells for food with inland Indians. On one such journey, he met up with three other survivors of his shipwrecked crew. Somehow the four Spaniards had earned reputations as healers. The Native Americans invited them into their villages and asked

them to treat their sick. One of the men was a black slave named Estéban. The Native Americans had never seen a black man before, and they believed Estéban had especially strong powers as a healer.

In 1536, Cabeza de Vaca and his men entered northern Mexico and met a party of Spaniards. His journey through the Gulf of Mexico region had lasted eight years and covered 6,000 miles (9,656 km). During this **trek,** he learned to respect and even love the Native American people. He wrote a book, *Adventures in the Unknown Interior of America,* which is exciting reading to this day. In the book, he details how the kindness of the Native Americans kept him alive during his long and difficult journey.

Francisco de Coronado, Explorer of the American Southwest

During the conquistador years, one exploring expedition often led to another. Spanish officials asked Cabeza de Vaca if he had seen any sign of rich cities as he trekked through the Gulf of Mexico region. He had seen nothing with his own eyes. But Cabeza de Vaca reported that Native Americans had told him that there were many rich cities in the north.

Just the hint of rich cities brought to life an old legend. The legend said seven Spanish priests journeyed across the

Cabeza de Vaca did not see any riches with his own eyes, but told Spanish officials that Native Americans had told him many stories of wealthy cities in the north.

Atlantic many years before Columbus. In the Americas, the priests found a region where gold was so plentiful the people used it as building material. The priests told of seven glorious cities built from bricks of pure gold. The legend called these places the Seven Cities of Cibola.

Imagine a city built from gold bricks such as these. That is what the Spanish explorers hoped to find in North America.

An expedition was formed to find the seven golden cities. Leading that expedition was Francisco de Coronado (1510–1554). Coronado was born in Salamanca, Spain. He was a handsome young man whose parents were friends of the Spanish king. In 1540, Coronado and 300 Spanish soldiers began their search for the Seven Cities of Cibola. With Coronado leading, the men marched out of New Spain toward the unknown lands to the north.

Coronado's men walked through the present-day U.S. states of Arizona and New Mexico. The black slave Estéban served as their guide. Sometimes the Spaniards fought Native American tribes. In one such clash, Estéban was killed. In August 1540, a group of Coronado's men encountered one of the most spectacular sights in the natural world—the Grand Canyon of Arizona. In their journals, however, not one Spaniard praised the canyon's beauty. Instead, the Spaniards complained that they wanted to drink the water of the Colorado River, which flowed below them, but the canyon's walls were too steep to climb!

The Coronado party spent the winter of 1540–1541 at a base camp in what is now northern New Mexico.

Coronado set off in search of golden cities in 1540. He and his men were willing to travel through unknown and possibly dangerous territory to find the legendary cities.

The Grand Canyon is one of the world's most beautiful sights, but the Spaniards did not appreciate its beauty. Instead they complained that they could not reach the water of the Colorado River that flows through this magnificent canyon.

The men called the base camp Cibola, after the seven golden cities. The Spaniards often befriended the Native American people they met. The tribal name of one people was Teyas, which meant "friends" in their native language. The state of Texas was later named after the Teyas tribe. Another friendly group was called the Querechos. They were very curious about the Spaniards' horses. Years later, the Querechos were known as the Apaches, and they were the finest horse riders in the American West.

In the spring of 1541, Coronado and his men reached as far as present-day Kansas. Having found no rich cities, the expedition turned south, back to New Spain. The journey had lasted more than two years. The men had seen the Grand Canyon and other wonders of the American Southwest. They **ventured** into the Great Plains, where immense herds of buffalo blackened the grasslands. But they had found no gold at all, and their presence triggered wars between Native Americans and whites. Some of Coronado's

Coronado and his men traveled hundreds of miles on foot and explored much of the North American Southwest as they searched for cities of gold.

men attacked the Indians with hunting dogs. One of Coronado's officers, López de Cárdenas, ordered that 200 Pueblo Indians be burned at the stake.

Upon his return, a Spanish court put Coronado on trial for committing "great cruelties upon the natives of the land through which he passed." Coronado was pronounced innocent of all charges. López de Cárdenas spent seven years in prison for ordering his men to kill the Indians. Coronado suffered ill health for the rest of his life. He died in 1554 at the age of 44.

Legacy of the Conquistadores

The conquistador era lasted roughly 50 years, from 1500 to 1550. The Spaniards brought to the Americas a new religion, a new language, and eventually a new race. However, their reputation in history is stained. They were motivated largely by greed, and their treatment of conquered people was often horrifying.

Certainly the conquistadores altered the history of Central and South America. The conquerors carved out a great Spanish empire in those lands. The Spanish influence over Latin America remains to this day. Four hundred years ago, the conquistadores sailed the Atlantic seeking gold, glory, and God. They succeeded in transforming a continent to their image.

Hernando de Soto (1500?–1542) was a Spanish military officer who served with Pizarro during the conquest of the Incas. De Soto, it seemed, was the greatest gentleman among Pizarro's followers. When the Inca people met Pizarro's ransom demands, de Soto argued that the Inca chief should be released. Pizarro refused to listen to de Soto, and the Inca leader was put to death. Nevertheless, de Soto accepted his share of the ransom and became wealthy.

De Soto's gentlemanly nature faded when he commanded his own exploring party. In 1539, de Soto led his own expedition to the present-day U.S. state of Florida. With 600 men, he landed at what is now Tampa Bay. Finding no gold, he journeyed inland to the north and the west. He often waged war on the Native Americans. He also **plundered** villages and stole food. Sometimes he followed Pizarro's practice of seizing a tribal chief and holding him for ransom.

De Soto led his followers through what is now Florida, Georgia, South Carolina, North Carolina, Tennessee, Alabama, Mississippi, Arkansas, and Louisiana. In May 1541, de Soto and his men became the first Europeans to see the mighty Mississippi River. De Soto crossed the river into Arkansas. Finding no gold, he returned to the Mississippi. There he became feverish and died. His companions weighted down his body with rocks and buried it in the river. Today, the De Soto National Memorial in Bradenton, Florida, commemorates his mission of exploration.

711: The Moors invade the lands controlled by Spain.

1475?: Vasco Núñez de Balboa is born in the Spanish town of Jerez de los Caballeros.

1478?: Francisco Pizarro is born in the town of Trujillo, Spain.

1485: Hernando Cortés is born near the Spanish city of Salamanca.

1490?: Álvar Núñez Cabeza de Vaca is born in Spain.

1492: The Spanish king and queen send Christopher Columbus on a mission to reach the Orient by sailing around the world. Instead of reaching the Orient, Columbus finds the Americas.

1500?: Hernando de Soto is born in Spain.

1501: Balboa joins a Spanish expedition sailing for South America.

1502: Pizarro sets sail for the Americas.

1504: Cortés sets sail for the Americas.

1510: Francisco Vásquez de Coronado is born in Salamanca, Spain.

1513: Vasco Núñez de Balboa, a Spanish conquistador, becomes the first European to see the Pacific Ocean.

1517: A Spanish ship is blown off course and touches upon the shores of present-day Mexico.

1519: Hernando Cortés sails for Mexico in February. In November he and his men find the Aztec city of Tenochtitlán. Francisco Pizarro helps to establish Panama City, Spain's first outpost on the Pacific. Falsely accused of treason, Balboa is beheaded in the central square of the Spanish settlement of Acla.

1520: The Aztecs drive the Spanish out of Tenochtitlán on June 30.

1521: Cortés completes the conquest of the mighty Aztec Empire.

1528: Álvar Núñez Cabeza de Vaca is shipwrecked off the Gulf of Mexico and begins an eight-year journey through the Gulf region.

1532: Pizarro and his army march into the Inca city of Cajamarca in present-day Peru where they kill many Inca soldiers and capture their chief, Atahualpa.

1533: On August 29, Pizarro orders the death of Atahualpa by strangulation.

1535: Pizarro founds the city of Lima, Peru.

1539: An expedition led by Hernando de Soto begins its exploration in present-day Florida.

1540: Francisco Vásquez de Coronado leads an expedition into the American Southwest. In late August, a group of Coronado's men discovers the Grand Canyon.

1541: Hernando de Soto is the first European to see the Mississippi River. Coronado and his expedition reach as far as present-day Kansas without finding the Seven Cities of Cibola and decide to return to New Spain.

1542: Hernando de Soto dies and is buried in the Mississippi River.

1547: Hernando Cortés dies on December 2 in a small town near Seville, Spain.

1554: Coronado dies at the age of 44.

exquisitely (ex-SWIZ-it-lee) Something that is exquisitely designed is beautifully or artistically done. Spanish soldiers acquired a fortune in exquisitely carved gold jewelry.

impenetrable (im-PEH-nuh-truh-buhl) A place that is impenetrable is impossible to enter or penetrate. In some regions, the Spaniards found nothing but impenetrable jungle.

monarch (MON-ark) A monarch is a king or a queen. The conquistadores came to the Americas to serve God and the monarch and also to find riches.

mystical (MISS-ti-kuhl) Something that is mystical is mysterious or has a spiritual meaning. One legend told of El Dorado, a mystical king who powdered his body in gold dust every morning as if he were taking a bath.

plundered (PLUHN-durd) If something is plundered, it has many things stolen from it by force. De Soto often plundered villages and stole food.

trek (TREK) A trek is a long journey that is slow and difficult. During his trek, Cabeza de Vaca learned to respect and even love the Native American people.

ventured (VEN-churd) Someone who has ventured has done something that is risky or hasn't been done before. The conquistadores ventured into lands never before explored by Europeans.

Books

Cantor, Carrie Nichols. *Francisco Vasquéz de Coronado: The Search for Cities of Gold.* Chanhassen, Minn.: The Child's World, 2003.

DeAngelis, Gina. *Francisco Pizarro and the Conquest of the Inca.* Philadelphia: Chelsea House, 2001.

Gaines, Ann Graham. *Hernando de Soto and the Spanish Search for Gold in World History.* Berkeley Heights, N.J.: Enslow Publishers, 2002.

Gibbons, Faye, and Bruce Dupree (illustrator). *Hernando de Soto: A Search for Gold and Glory.* Birmingham, Ala.: Crane Hill Publishers, 2002.

Hinds, Kathryn. *The Incas.* New York: Benchmark Books, 1998.

Tanaka, Shelley. *The Lost Temple of the Aztecs: What It Was Like When the Spaniards Invaded Mexico.* New York: Hyperion Press, 1998.

Web Sites

Visit our Web page for lots of links about the conquistadores:
http://www.childsworld.com/links.html

Note to parents, teachers, and librarians: We routinely check our Web links to make sure they're safe, active sites—so encourage your readers to check them out!

About the Author

R. Conrad Stein was born in Chicago, Illinois. At age 18, he enlisted in the U.S. Marines and served for three years. He later attended the University of Illinois and earned a degree in history. Mr. Stein is a full-time writer. Over the years, he has published more than 150 books, mostly history and geography titles. The author was especially pleased to write for A Proud Heritage because he lived in Mexico for seven years during the 1970s. The Stein family still spends most of the summer months in the town of San Miguel de Allende in central Mexico. The rest of the year, Mr. Stein lives in Chicago with his wife, children's book author Deborah Kent, and their daughter, Janna.